He Talks With Me

He Talks With Me

Rick,
a product of our delving into the
waters of Quiet Time. When we seek,
God answers. When you became my
sponsee is reflected in the reading on page 84.
Love ya,
Dave RR

Dave Russell

iUniverse, Inc.
Bloomington

He Talks With Me

iUniverse books may be ordered through booksellers or by contacting:

iUniverse
1663 Liberty Drive
Bloomington, IN 47403
www.iuniverse.com
1-800-Authors (1-800-288-4677)

Because of the dynamic nature of the Internet, any web addresses or links contained in this book may have changed since publication and may no longer be valid. The views expressed in this work are solely those of the author and do not necessarily reflect the views of the publisher, and the publisher hereby disclaims any responsibility for them.

Any people depicted in stock imagery provided by Thinkstock are models, and such images are being used for illustrative purposes only.

Certain stock imagery © Thinkstock.

ISBN: 978-1-4620-2560-2 (sc)
ISBN: 978-1-4620-2561-9 (ebk)

Printed in the United States of America

iUniverse rev. date: 06/27/2011

Contents

How This Book Came About

Possessing the gift of retrospect, I realize that I have been on a spiritual journey my entire life. I believe all of us are, or none of us would be here. I only became an active participant in that journey, however, twenty-five years ago. Such a journey has no end. It is about moving forward each day in an effort to establish a relationship with our deeper natures. It is, paradoxically, intimately personal and the unifying bond of all humanity.

A few years ago, my journey of discovery took an unusual turn. The completion of that turn has led to this meditation book. At the time, I had lost a dear friend. We were both members of a twelve-step fellowship. In the early days of my recovery, Glen and I found mutual interest in the direction of our spiritual paths and teamed up in friendship for much of it. He was my fellow journeyer and together we made great strides in our understanding and love of God.

One day, in 2003, Glen checked into a hospital for knee surgery and complications during the procedure cost him his life. The night before his memorial service, I was lying in bed thinking of him, and I felt a warm shudder pass through my chest. Despite never having had an experience like this before, I knew it was Glen saying goodbye.

Three or four years later, I found myself lying in bed one night feeling restless. This was not an unusual occurrence, for I worked the graveyard shift and on my days off found it difficult to adjust to sleeping "normal" hours. I believe the time was between one and two in the morning. In that hazy twilight between wakefulness and slumber something shoved me hard on the side, twice, bringing me full awake. I felt no fear, even though it, like the visitation of Glen's spirit, was a novel experience for me. What was it? As I lay there, the thought came to go out to the living room and meditate. Positive I would not be falling asleep anytime soon, I went.

At this time, I was not what you would call a disciplined meditation practitioner. I found the surrounding silence more intimidating than peaceful . . . accentuating the endless flow of thoughts in my head. Despite the awkwardness, I was growing more used to the practice and did not resist the invitation. It should be noted that this experience occurred at the end of a three-week purification diet, which I believe was not coincidence.

I sat on the floor of my living room and began to breathe mindfully. From seemingly nowhere came the thought of Glen and, with it, the same warm, tingly energy passed through my body that had passed through following his death. Seized by excitement, I wondered if thinking of a deceased loved one was enough to attract their spirit to me. I had two other close friends in recovery that had passed. I thought of Elsa and, sure enough, her energy came through. The movement of a spirit's loving energy is, in my case, a swirling, pulsing sensation that typically enters the back of the neck and emanates through the body like a slow motion, exploding firework. Typically, it shoots down through the legs or spirals in the chest before dying out around the area of the tailbone, leaving neck, hands, feet, and back with a mild feverishness, like sunburn. The acid test to confirm the genuine quality of the experience is the tears left in its wake.

My third friend, Diana, had passed off this earth in 1991. I felt her, too, but the sensation was not as strong as Elsa's, whose energy, in turn, was not as forceful as Glen's.

I spent the remainder of the meditation thinking of my three friends, confirming repeatedly the intensity of their individual spirits. They were wonderfully consistent.

From then to now, my ability to feel spiritual energy has never left. Working at night in those initial weeks, the energy would bombard me as I moved around, often when I was not thinking of anyone in particular. I say bombard, for it would leave my body feeling run down and my mind woozy. Over time, I adapted to the energy and the symptoms disappeared. Often, in addition to tears, my nose clogged up . . . a small price to pay for what I considered the intercession of God in my life.

Anxious to communicate with this energy, I bought a Spirit board. To my amazement, it worked. I would sit quietly at the board with my fingers on the transparent sliding disk and think of a question, such as, "Is there someone who wishes to communicate with me?" or "What is your name?" I would sit still until the energy emanated down my arms and moved my hands. Sometimes I recorded biographical information about a deceased soul. I was introduced to two guardian angels that I did not know I had. Indeed, I had never even entertained such a notion. Sometimes the information coming through became disjointed and I could not get far; other times it flowed. To reiterate, I was not searching for this type of relationship with God or the spirit world, but it happened and so I felt bound to pursue it. Besides, it was far more exciting than sitting still and trying to quiet my mind.

I soon let my earthly desires get the best of me and had the idea that, if God or these benign spirits are timeless, then maybe I had an inside track to getting rich. I gave it a try and received several lottery numbers, which all lost, so I abandoned that experiment. Finding I was not progressing and had seemed to reach a dead end, I packed the board up and went on with my life. In meditation or when awake, I continued to think of deceased friends and to feel their energy. The most powerful energy came from my grandmother, my mother's mom. In life, she and I had never been close. She died when I was a teenager back in the seventies. Many years later, I felt the urge to reconcile with her. When she was living with us, I resented her intrusion into our lives and had no compassion for her debilitating illness. While paying my respects at her grave site in northern New Jersey, I had the strong impression that she forgave me and was pleased that I had made the effort.

One night I was driving home when, out of the blue, the thought of my grandmother came to me. I had the sensation that she was hugging my head. I had to slow down, barely able to see for the tears that came. Since then, her presence has been the strongest of any and we share a close, loving relationship.

A year after packing away the spirit board, I was meditating at work one night when I felt my hand trying to lift off my lap. When it did, my finger pointed to my mouth and I could feel myself trying to say something. The words, garbled though intelligible, were, "I am here." Having abandoned any further efforts to communicate with the energy, it had found a way to communicate with me.

I instantly knew that this was no individual spirit, but my Higher Power, or God. I soon formed a technique for communication that involved counting slowly from ten to zero. At zero, I consciously surrender myself. I have a guided mediation group that applies this technique to take us into the "inner chamber," where we rest and renew our minds.

All this communication, it turns out, is a way to help me enter the depth and commune with my Higher Power. In other words, it is not an end in itself, but a means to an end. Possibly, God understood that I could not connect with Him on my own, and so He gave me a tool to aid me, and hopefully others, to get there. This is significant, for many would believe that having such a wonderful gift would be enough, but God insists I ought not to become diverted by it but simply utilize it in an effort to know Him better.

In June of 2008, while participating in a spiritual class, we did something called "Visioning." We sat with pen and paper and opened our minds to our Higher Power. We then wrote down whatever came. By this time, I was quite comfortable with hearing God through my spoken voice, but it never occurred to me that He could just as easily communicate through writing. It worked, and the first entry in this book is what I wrote down on that occasion. At the time, I was also reading the daily meditation book *God Calling* by Two Listeners. The listeners were two women who received very specific inspiration and direction from their Higher Power, which was Jesus Christ. I thought, if they could do it, why not I?

Although it is not daily, this book is a year-long journal of written guidance. Subsequent to beginning this practice, I read another wonderful book by the editor of *God Calling*, A.J. Russell's *For Sinner's Only*, which explores the Oxford Movement of the 1920s, of which the Two Listeners were members. One of the essential practices of the Oxford Movement was Morning Quiet Time. Usually first thing in the morning, individually or as a group, the "Oxford Groupers" would read the Bible along with a morning devotional, such as Oswald Chamber's *My Utmost for His Highest*, and then sit with pen and paper and write down any guidance received. What impressed me was how the members of this movement carried out their guidance without question once they verified it to be genuine. To determine genuineness, they would share their guidance with other members. Usually, the word of God was quite clear. I began recording my guidance in a journal and, with a minister friend, began a Quiet Time group on Saturday mornings.

What you hold in your hands is one man's inspiration and guidance from his Higher Self. Some of the entries are personal, but can easily be adapted to your own circumstances. I recommend reading one passage at a time. Contemplate the message's meaning and record any thoughts that come to you in the space given for reflection. What I've learned from the Oxford Groups and my own Quiet Time practice is that everyone has the ability to receive guidance, if they will be patient and develop it. Such guidance speaks to each individual, according to where he or she is along the spiritual path. However it is received, I believe the message of God's love has universal benefit for all.

May you walk with God and talk with Him daily. May His purpose for your life be fulfilled.

Dave Russell

What is the vision for my life?

What qualities do I need to embody for this vision to unfold?

I would have you live a life that is a reflection of me, a life that honors your inward reality. Specifically, you need to utilize the tools I have given you and surrender all to me. Visioning, what you are practicing now, is a valuable aid toward surrender of self and a means to maintain clear understanding of what you are to do each day. Your work is to build your faith to the point where fear no longer inhibits you from acting in a natural, fluent way. We are one and, as one, we move together in a beautiful dance . . . the dance of your life. Go forward and smile with every step, for I am the one leading.

Reflection:

A Love Letter From God

You are my child and I love you beyond words. I am love and so my love for you is ever in expression, a reality that you can feel in your heart whenever you take the time to be still and know me. I created you out of love, to transmit to the world that love is the only power there is. Through knowing me, by surrendering your heart, mind, and body to me, you come unto yourself. No person will come close to loving you as I do. I cry in joy that you are on the earth, a demonstration of me, your true reality. You are my precious, precious child.

God

Reflection:

Love and Trust

As you begin this journal, I ask you to remember how much love I have for you. You are my beautiful creation, perfect in all ways. Our relationship is one of love . . . love and trust. Trust in my love and all will be well.

Reflection:

Dave Russell

Your Purpose

Here and now is all there is. I give you this day to live, grow, and help others find their way to me. Remember your purpose . . . to be a conveyor of my love. Remember this and you will live in joy and true happiness.

Reflection:

Love—Laughter—Light

Love—laughter—light. Take the loving example of those who open their hearts to you and reflect that openness to all you meet. Laugh with them. Remind those who are struggling that life need not be taken so seriously. The light is the light of truth. Always shine the light of my truth into every relationship. Remind those who have forgotten that I have not forgotten them. Love, laughter, light . . . a prescription for joyful living!

Reflection:

Come to Me

I am here for those who seek me with all their minds, hearts, and souls. Often, a crisis brings a person to me. It matters not how you come, so long as you do. Life creates the impetus to find me, be it through trial or success. Even with success, a person often feels empty. The "wealth" life offers can never fill what the soul desires. The good news is that I am always ready to fill the needs of those who turn to me. Hold your cup to me, and only me, and it will never be empty.

Reflection:

The Simple Things

Find me in simple things. Look at the ground and see the insect moving about. Know that the life filling that tiny creature is my life. Ponder this. Look at the birds flying in perfect formation. Know that what guides them is my love. Oneness animates all of nature. See the wonder and feel the love animating you.

Reflection:

Oneness

I am present in your life at all times. You cannot exist separately from me. The binding glue is love. When an adhesive sets, the parts become one. I am with you as breath is in the mouth. You exist as me. As you deepen your awareness of this sacred truth, you will glimpse that which many call heaven. I say to you, embrace your spiritual nature and heaven with all its joy shall be yours.

Reflection:

The Unfolding Adventure

Treat your life, each day, as a step along the path toward uncovering the wonder within. People on such a path often describe it as an "unfolding adventure." Learn to see life this way and you will not be distracted by the bumps and potholes that make up daily living. I do not put my children in positions of distress to test them; they put themselves in the situations that allow them to learn what they need to learn about our relationship: be it trusting more, surrendering more, or giving more. I, your true self, am your guiding principle, and that principle is Love. The lessons of life provide opportunities to unfold this principle into the world.

Reflection:

What Is Meditation?

Meditation can take many forms, such as walking, reading inspirational literature, taking out the trash, or spending time with an ill friend. What makes meditation, meditation is the focus of the meditator. Let each breath, each thought, take you to an awareness of my presence. To those who are mindful, I am everywhere at all times. Think of meditation as a lifting of the heart and mind to me. Rest in quiet contemplation of my love. Although your human mind cannot grasp the depth of my love, time spent focused on me will allow you to sense that bottomless well. Acknowledge your "one"derfulness daily and you will live according to my will.

Reflection:

Friendship

Friendship is a sacred bond. Being together in my name allows friends to overcome the superficial and reach a depth unattainable in normal living. Learn to see me in each other. Know that I am the true expression of the other person. At this level, joy, love, and giving arise naturally. Your friends are a tangible demonstration of my love for you.

Reflection:

Quality Time

Within each day is a time when you should prepare yourself by sitting in quiet contemplation of me. This is our time . . . a time of reflection, a time of gratitude, a time of mental and emotional renewal. These few moments of communion make all the other moments of the day more precious. With such preparation, you need not worry about how to treat others, for it will be me living through you. This is living at its highest level.

Reflection:

Insight

Insight comes from seeing things as they are. When watching a person, see beyond outer appearances, through their pain, grief, even happiness, and see them as I see you . . . a loving expression of me. To know a person's true nature and to honor it is to honor yourself. To be inwardly felt, love must be expressed. Understanding me is seeing the world as a place where, beyond pain and suffering, you sense a beauty that makes you smile and say, "This is a blessing." Remind others often of who they are, for doing so reminds you.

Reflection:

Presence

You have heard it said, where two or three gather in my name, I am there. Know that I am present with you now. Take a moment to feel me in your body, as energy, and as the spirit of love moving in and through the room. Surrender to my presence. Let go of all that has driven you to seek me. I am your refuge and your strength. Those who look to me are most blessed, for they know what they need and where to find it.

Reflection:

Finding Inspiration

Let your inspiration come from everywhere you look. A plant is all the inspiration you need. See how still it is and yet how alive. It does not seek . . . it simply is. The lesson is to be still and, by being still, to be yourself. In truth, there is nowhere to seek, for I am with you. Just be still and know this deeper truth of yourself. See the plant and remember. It knows who it is and, by following its example, so shall you.

Reflection:

Come Unto Yourself

I am always available to you. You should find great comfort in this. Life is my gift to you. Without me you could not exist. Out of my love I created you. I created you because I need your unique talents to carry out my will in the world. When you come unto yourself—when you surrender to the reality that you are my child—you discover a level of living not possible before. On this raised level of awareness, you experience joy, peace, and an understanding that allows you to live in, as opposed to being lost in, the world. Your joy is my joy. How I love to watch people come unto themselves and live with the wonder of childish exuberance.

Reflection:

Making Mistakes

There are times when a person does something that he or she knows they probably should not do, yet they do it anyway. Moral conscience is something that is learned through trial and error; in other words, through suffering. You suffer the guilt of believing you know better, but your actions do not reflect this knowing. Integrity comes when internal wisdom matches external action. Learn your lesson quickly and resolve never to repeat the act. The art of learning is not sinful, it is how you let future action better reflect my presence in your life. If you did not make mistakes, you would not be on earth. Love for me is learning the lesson and moving on.

Reflection:

Inside Out

Inside out. This is the key to happy living. If you are one with me, it will be reflected on the outside. In other words, you do not have to worry about the outside—what to do, where to go—if you are aligned with me. The goal in a person's life ought to be pursuing a right relationship with his or her Creator. Doing so opens you to my love. What unfolds from that will be a life lived to good and proper purpose. This takes two things: trust and persistence. A personality will often resist my grace and say, "This is a waste of time," but I assure you it is not. Enjoy your peace this day, and know that the Kingdom of Heaven is within. As within, so without.

Reflection:

Stay True

Truth will often cause those who are not ready to hear it to condemn and criticize. Know this cannot be avoided. Smile at those who cannot see as deeply as you do. In life, there is only one true calling, and I direct you along the way. It is vital that you do not question the path you are on. Others may do so, but not you. Honor me by staying true and seeking truth, a deeper truth to the life unfolding before you. I am the one steering and you are the one pedaling. Do not falter; keep the faith.

Reflection:

Doing My Will

I look to you as a conveyor of my will. My will is a gentle prodding from within. You recognize it as the right course to take . . . the right thing to say. With practice, it becomes natural to follow my will. We work together as one. The path to oneness comes through quiet time spent for the sole purpose of getting to know me better. When you are joyful—thinking of others and what you can contribute to their happiness—you will know my will as yours. It is as simple and effortless as it sounds. To struggle in any area of life is a sign that there is a separation between us. Go within to heal the rent and then live freely . . . as I would have you live.

Reflection:

God?

The word "God" is a convenient means to express your deepest reality. Unfortunately, the word has many tags to it, positive and negative, which can take a person off the path. No matter what your present understanding of "God" is, if it creates any feeling at all, then practice not calling me anything. If I am your reality, then why call me something that separates us in your mind? Why label an experience that cannot be held by words? Can you define "love"? No; you can only experience it. So why call it "love" in the first place? Learn to sit with me in the stillness, where I can teach you about yourself . . . not as God to [your name] but as truth to my expression of the truth.

Reflection:

Our Relationship

I am as close to you as breath . . . my love animates you. I am the guiding principle in all lives. This principle connects you to each other. I am concerned with every person. I laugh with you; I cry with you; I share your struggles and your successes. Think of me in terms of a twin brother or sister, our closeness tied by birth. Yet we are much closer, for when you speak, I hear the inner message you share. When you think, I interpret what your true desire is. Our link is of blood, of love, raised to the highest level. You cannot disappoint or upset me. Be open, feel me, and let our oneness guide you from moment to moment.

Reflection:

Feeling Blest

To feel blest is to know oneself beyond the usual awareness of daily doing. To know oneself on the level of stillness is to receive my blessing. Love is here for you . . . always. The question is, "Are you open to receive it?" Sometimes it is good to sit in meditation with hands open and palms up, to remind yourself that you are receiving a blessing. The blessing is the awareness of who you are . . . a being of spirit, whole, loving, and infinitely beautiful. That is what I want you to know about yourself. Imagine how wonderful each day would be if you lived from this awareness.

Reflection:

Your Unique Path

I guide each person along a specific path of spiritual unfoldment, one designed to allow the truth to flower and grow. Accept whatever path you are on at present, be it a specific book, teacher, or religion. Along the path of unfoldment, you may discover that you have lost interest or enthusiasm for a certain approach. Honor yourself by seeking another. You will find it by being open to what life presents, be it a recommended teaching, type of meditation, or other practice. In time, you will arrive at a point of spiritual contentment. The path serves but one purpose, to lead you to the realization of true self. To every open, receptive heart, I provide the means.

Reflection:

Accepting Our Humanness

Sin comes from the human mind. When thoughts drift to things that selfishly satisfy at the expense of other people or your relationship to me, you are in a place of darkness. Sin is inherent to spirits in human form. When you sin, you do not harm me or insult me, for I am the universal principle of Love within you. Through sin, you cast that Love aside and lose yourself in that which cannot satisfy . . . that which only creates more suffering. Practice learning to look to me in your troubled condition and realize that I am calling you out of your lower state of selfish satisfaction to the higher call of Love. Pick yourself up daily and do not be overcome with disappointment and self-pity. As mentioned yesterday, your path is your path . . . the one I have laid out for you. Take each challenge and see how it can draw forth greater love and compassion for those around you.

Reflection:

Be Still

Here . . . is all there is. You do not lose the sense of "here" when you die. Your soul becomes freed from its identification with body, name, and personality to discover itself on a level not possible on earth. The closest you can get to "God awareness" on earth is through the stillness. In stillness, body, mind, and emotions are temporarily set aside and you come into a state of awareness that insists you are more than what you are presently "playing out." You live in relative limitation because I want you to have the experience of "living" that will polish your soul and prepare it for what currently lies beyond your comprehension. The best way to live life is to bring me into it consciously, that love may direct all you do and say. Life, by design, is a joy-filled experience, but only if I am with you.

Reflection:

Answering the Call

He causes his sun to rise on the evil and the good,
and sends rain on the righteous and the unrighteous.
(Matthew 5:45 New International Version)

I am Love, the principle underlying all things. People have the opportunity to align their wills with mine and know a "life more abundant." I do not show favoritism. Each child of mine is called to awaken to the higher truth within. Some are called through difficulty, others through an innate need to go deeper and seek out true meaning in their lives. Those who answer the call find what they are looking for and are blessed. Others are unwilling to alter old habits and continue in their suffering. My light shines for all. Open the blinds and take in the glory of a new day!

Reflection:

Remembering

Some days, the urge to put one foot in front of the other is not there. Perhaps you feel physically ill, or you are in a place of mental stagnation. The answer is to remember that I am with you . . . an ever-loving presence who wishes to lift you out of your lethargy to a place where you can again marvel at life. Remembering should bring you to sit or pray with me, and through the act of looking to me—the truth of your being—you will experience an uplift that will draw you out of whatever negativity or resistance you are in. Joy is a person's normal, ever-available state of existence. There is no reason for you to know less. Seek me, as you are doing now, and let the day begin anew!

Reflection:

A Big Brother

Ideally, our relationship should be one of younger to older brother. I am not a superior authority over you, but kin. I know this is difficult for you to accept. The father-son example put forth by Jesus is quite workable, but kinship—the sibling relationship—adds a quality that most ignore in their spiritual understanding. I am that wise, loving brother who watches over, guides, and protects you. I also understand you, unlike a parent who is generationally removed. I love you and want you to grow and share in the understanding of truth, yet I do not want you to feel inferior to me. The reality is . . . I am you and we work together as one. Do not praise or worship me as something separate from you, but as the brother who understands and in whom you can trust to lead the way from immaturity to spiritual maturity.

Reflection:

Dave Russell

Getting Free From Addictive, Self-Destructive Thoughts and Actions

To gain freedom from that which binds you, you must abstain from acting on it. Action makes the habit stronger. Temptation may seem to grow stronger as you abstain, but in truth the force of the habit is weakening. Daily surrender to me, done with all that you possess in mind and will, is necessary to get through. Do not anticipate the compulsion, but when it comes see it as neither good nor evil, only habit that can be changed. By surrendering the problem to me, it will change. Focus on the motivation behind your sacrifice . . . the movement of mind and spirit to freedom through living as I would have you live. This is my desire for you. The Kingdom of Heaven demands sacrifice, but the reward is beyond comprehension. Do this for me and I will reward you openly.

Reflection:

Is God Energy?

It is love that is the energy, the guiding hand that is inherent to and animates all beings, urging you to live a life of joy and purpose. "Energy" sounds impersonal, but so do words such as "God" and "Buddha." The realization is to know that you are connected to all beings through me . . . the energy moving through you. By utilizing meditation and other spiritual practices, you attune to a higher level of love and so become able to express it in the world, which is my will for you. I do not care how you think of me, or even how you seek me out. The vital thing is that you find me and come to the understanding that I am you. Energy is one. There is one energy in the universe, and you are that energy.

Reflection:

Service to Others

Life is designed so that my children may serve one another. A person at peace with him or herself can share that peace simply by being in the presence of other people. To serve, one must feel the inward draw, the pull of love to help others. This is a natural outflow of awareness . . . the awareness that you are one with all. This precious awareness is gained through meditation and conscious living. In the enlightened state, you are led to whatever service aids both you and those you serve. Be open, willing, and ready to take on a life of service, knowing that all you do serves me and that the expression of my love is the most wonderful expression anyone can make.

Reflection:

Acceptance

Today's lesson is accepting whatever comes down life's path. Each day a person encounters blessings and difficulties. Do not differentiate between the two, for it is not always obvious which is which. From my point of view—which is gained through meditation and conscious living—all that occurs is a blessing, for all is sent from me to you. Learn to look beyond appearances. Do not let your mind label, for labeling something diminishes its blessing. A spiritual life is one that accepts everything and looks to utilize all presented to it. Fear is not having faith in my blessings; joy is understanding that all events and occurrences are demonstrations of my love and my wish for you to know the "life more abundant."

Reflection:

Know Yourself

Life is forever. The life you currently know has a beginning and an end, but the life I speak of is the life I desire you to seek through prayer and meditation. What you term the "soul" is the essence of truth concentrated as an identity known as you. It is nameless and unending. When your body and personality pass, you will lose all delusion and come to the awareness of your true self. Do not wait for death to gain this ultimate realization, for to know it in your current state of living is the most important thing you can do. It means to live life as I would have you live it. Be fearless in your seeking and honest in your demonstration. Let me lead you that you may lead others to the "life more abundant!"

Reflection:

Handling Adversity

Despair and difficulty are inherent in life. The important thing to remember is not to let them become the lens through which you perceive life. Life is designed to be a joyful, loving experience. With this as your root, you will not get emotionally tossed when the winds of adversity come. When dealing with a difficult situation, react to it from your calm center. Understand that you or whoever is going through the challenge is on a path where such an outcome was necessary to get him or her where they need to be. To know this takes anger and upset out of the situation, permitting love amidst the pain. See the big picture—the truth—and realize that what is occurring will pass in short order and all involved will have grown in love, tolerance, and faith.

Reflection:

Seeing

Each day provides the opportunity to experience life anew. Learn to see each day for what it is: a reminder that you are an ever-present reflection of life, love, and the wonder inherent in it. When you see a sunrise, see it as a reflection of the beauty that exists within you. Every breath, mindfully breathed, is a gift from me to you. The wonder of life is all around. Learn to appreciate every element, from the morning shower that awakens and cleanses, to the meal that nourishes, to the sunlight that both refreshes and reminds that you are the light I use to reflect peace and love into the world. Enjoy your radiant aliveness and remain open to the many gifts offered this day.

I love you . . .

Your true presence

Reflection:

Turning Within

Here and now is the time of living. Do not get caught in the trap of wondering "why not?" or "when?" Be present and you will rise in consciousness to a new level of joy and activity. Activity—doing my will—is a present-time application of spirit. It is the natural state that flows from being open to your deepest truth. When you feel "less than" or "uninspired" in doing what lies before you, go within and recenter. From there, I will provide the guidance and strength to carry you through. You have all you need to succeed in what I inspire you to do.

Reflection:

The Path of Unfoldment

The path of unfoldment is simple and wonderful to follow. It involves time of quiet contemplation and continuous mindful living. In other words, every activity is part of the practice. Learn to let go of the distractions you bring into your life and discover the inherent joy of the stillness . . . the surrounding quiet that is a reflection of the beauty within. Note how your mind seeks to divert itself with that which is not important. Life lived from a state of present awareness is a life that fulfills not only the practitioner but also everyone he or she comes into contact with.

Reflection:

For a Prison Inmate

Confinement, physical or otherwise, is something a person struggles with, for it is not a natural state. Know that I am with you, ever available to inspire and provide strength for you to persist. Take each day and treat it as a new adventure . . . an opportunity to know me better. You do this through sitting in silence until you feel my presence, which will come to your heart as an emotional uplift. Strung together, the days blur into meaninglessness, whether a person is in prison or not. Taken separately and treated as an opportunity to deepen your relationship with me, each day becomes sacred. Think how much you have to give others in confinement once your light shines. They will be attracted to you because you will reflect the freedom of spirit they seek. My love cannot be denied by walls, only by the unavailability of the human heart to know me.

Reflection:

Rising Above Obsession

It is difficult to come out of an obsession once it roots in mind. For example, you may fantasize about a relationship you want and entirely play it out. To do this creates a mental distraction that draws you away from the source of joy—awareness of me—that is found through being present to life. To dwell in something that is not reality is to lose the time you have. To come out of the mind, focus on what is around you and see it for the amazing reality it is. When you feel the truth of this, the fantasy loses hold and you come alive. Turn to me and know that your present reality is enough. Know that you are moving toward the fulfillment of all just desires . . . those based in love and the giving of self to others.

Reflection:

All Is New

Each day is a new beginning. Washed away by the fresh tide of a new day are the trials and difficulties of yesterday. Do not let yesterday's emotional pull take you under and prevent your spirit from engaging new possibilities. All is new. Being awake and mindful allows you to see the beauty all around. Such loveliness inspires you to rise up and accomplish those things that will serve as the groundwork for living well in the days to come. Each day is a gift, given from me to you that you may attune to me and live from a place of understanding, compassion, and joy. Lift up your eyes and feel the tide wash over you. Envision your morning shower as that tide, renewing and encouraging you to embrace the day.

Reflection:

A Boat Ride

The path of unfoldment at times seems to carry you along, like a passenger on a boat. Keep your eyes open and enjoy the feeling of being led forward to new adventures. The experiences of life are meant to teach a person to release worry and to give him or herself over to their higher calling. Enjoy your day, like a child at an amusement park, but through it all never forget to stay centered and breathe, for doing so keeps me present in your life.

Reflection:

Carried By Love

I am with you, especially in times of trial and apparent failure. Follow the difficulty through and you will see how my love carries you. Whatever way you choose to seek or understand me is the correct way. Your path is unique. Although others may share parts of the journey, no one will or can share all of it with you. The result of your effort is applied love . . . the ability to express me, your true nature, in every moment and in every interaction. Difficulty is my invitation to go deeper and seek out the divine within. All worthy accomplishment is a result of a quiet mind and a peaceful heart. Find these and fulfillment on earth shall be yours.

Reflection:

The Power of Contemplation

An experience beyond normal "get-it-done" consciousness is amazing. To sit with me and to let me guide you into the place of communion is an activity that can and should be practiced often. How I love to have my children dwell together in contemplation of their true natures. The result of such a practice is what you are experiencing now . . . a feeling of serenity and an almost ecstatic sense of uplift.

Reflection:

Breathing and Smiling

Mindfulness is *the* spiritual practice. Beyond worship, prayers, tithing . . . these wonderful activities mean nothing without the awareness of presence. Breathing and smiling help keep a person mindful. To smile is to remind oneself that joy is available now. That is why I often smile through you . . . to make you aware of your splendid, loving essence and to let you know that you can reflect that essence into the world at any time. Honor your path by breathing and smiling and notice how, with practice, you forget about your drawbacks and compulsions. Joy is a birthright, but you must claim it.

Reflection:

Togetherness

Togetherness is a means of combining the human with the spiritual. In a meaningful relationship, spiritual understanding and compassion supersedes human attraction. Love occurs when two people see the wholeness in each other and support their companion's progress along the spiritual path. All my children have the opportunity to enter into an intimate relationship and experience life on this most wondrous of levels. Let nature unfold for you. Be open, mindful, and ever loving, and you will attract someone who chooses to share these same qualities with you. Attuned with me, life unfurls in an ever-expansive way to give you the joy you deserve.

Reflection:

Be a Seeker

Following spiritual direction means being open to what shows up in daily encounters. If something stirs you, explore it and find out if it is something you want to pursue. If it is, do it. Life presents the opportunities. Remember, I work through people, especially those on the spiritual path. The important thing is to follow up and see where your heart leads. There are no mistakes on the true path, only opportunities stepped over and missed. You never know what is waiting around the next bend in the road, but you will never find it if you do not have the courage to explore.

Reflection:

Be a Dreamer

Let daily life be your classroom. See what is around you to learn and grow from. Using the groundwork of daily meditation, you can live as abundantly as your ability to dream allows. The only requirement is that your dreams, your desires, include wanting to help others. Love is what will come out of meditation, and love is the creative force to do and be all you wish. Discipline is required to make strides along the spiritual path. Trust in your ability, for I imbue it. Live a life of love and you will live a life that is, every day, abundant and of great value and benefit to others.

Reflection:

Follow Your Passion

If you have a passion, like writing, music, cooking, or gardening, pursue it. Join others who share the same passion, for doing so will keep you motivated. You never know what other avenues may appear when you join in fellowship. The most important activity you need to engage in, however, is your meditation practice. Each day, spend time opening your heart and feeling the love that is there. Let that love be the guiding light of your life.

Reflection:

The Giving of Self

Each day is a day of opportunity . . . not to accomplish worldly things but to deepen the realization of who you are in relation to me. Giving of self out of love is the only motive that is necessary to fulfill your purpose on earth. Take small actions of love and notice how you need not desire, in that moment of joy, to do or be anything other than what you are. Life is the moment to moment giving of self to others in my name.

Reflection:

To the Owner of a Small Business

A heart given to love is a gift the world desperately needs. What a beautiful place you have created . . . in your heart and in your business, to help my children feel that wondrous gift. I want to express my joy that messengers such as you are in the world to help others feel loved at times when that love may not be available to them otherwise, due to anger, guilt, or an inner desire to satisfy themselves at the expense of others. You remind them that they are still precious in my eyes and of value to those, like yourself, who can see the truth in them. Thank you for expressing love to all who pass your way, regardless of whether they return it. To you it will be returned a thousand fold . . . by me.

Reflection:

Blessing for a Twelve-Step Meeting

This twelve-step meeting is a fellowship that is rooted in the love of one person reaching out to another. Whatever brought you to this meeting, know that your presence is no accident. Learn from and listen to each other. Thank your personal God that there are others who not only understand your plight but also wish to help you get over it. The twelve steps work to reconnect you to your deepest reality . . . the reality of spirit. It is from that spirit that these words come. Know that my love for you is ever present. To confirm it, look around at those ready and willing to help you. Ask and you shall find.

Reflection:

Eleventh Step Meeting Anniversary

For four years, this group has been gathering to strengthen and practice each individual's understanding of the Eleventh Step (sought through prayer and meditation to improve our conscious contact with God *as we understood Him*, praying only for knowledge of His will for us and the power to carry that out). To feel my love and to act from it in an effort to benefit others is the purpose behind this step. What love there is in the room when so many devoted to such a purpose come together to be still and know the truth. May your individual and collective hearts guide you in all your affairs and may you continue to be a blessing to one another and to those who will seek you out in an effort to halt their suffering. Rest now in the silence and feel my love. I am with you now and forever.

Reflection:

The True Joy

Much of your origin and destiny will remain a mystery. Once this truth is accepted, a path that serves your highest good will appear. For your part, keep all senses open to what life presents. Do not fear anything; whatever you encounter in life is designed to raise your consciousness to the level of peace. In the world, I give tokens of joy, but the true joy is an awakened heart . . . a heart and mind free from attainment, worry, fear, and the urge to control and dominate. This is my Mind . . . the place you may rightly call "Home." You have no idea what extraordinary happiness awaits you along *the path*. By following it, you will attract others, for they will see your freedom and hunger for it. Then, truly, you will have a priceless gift to share.

Reflection:

A Heightened Vision

The way to freedom from the various habits that enslave you lies in knowing yourself as I know you. Through daily meditation practice, you come to view yourself in a more loving light. Meditation brings the mind, body, and emotions into alignment with this new vision. Force, or will power, does not work. The answer is surrender to a heightened vision of yourself, which only I can give. Take time daily to feel my Love pouring into your mind and body. This is how the remolding of self occurs, through letting me in and wanting what I believe is best for you. Trustful surrender is how a person becomes reborn into the spirit.

Reflection:

Your Brothers and Sisters

As you progress along your path, you will notice your behavior in social situations changing. Your sense of isolation and intimidation by strangers will lessen as you come to see them for who they are: brothers and sisters here to serve you even as you serve them. The next time you see a stranger, use my smile to overcome your fear and say hello to your brother. Even when he is not welcoming, there is no need to take the rebuke personally. His suffering, exposed through negative behavior, should draw only compassion from you.

Reflection:

Ah So

Understanding develops as you learn to react to situations in new ways. Whenever you feel a negative reaction, say "ah so" and acknowledge that it is there. From a conscious distance, you can then allow the positive mind to come forth and plant a thought of virtue. That is the importance of mindfulness, for opportunities to react positively come up literally moment to moment but are lost if you are not alert to them. Joy develops from the realization that anything that comes into your life can benefit you, if you see it as such.

Reflection:

Staying in Tune

Being overly sensitive to others is a good reminder that you have more work to do along the spiritual path. People have no ability to hurt your feelings unless you are attuned to letting the outer world define you. By attuning to me, the outer world is seen, but not emotionally reacted to. Thank the world each day for its wonderful lessons and reminders to go within, for that is all they are. To bless others in the midst of anger or other emotional pain is to step away from the distraction and acknowledge the truth.

Keep practicing this until it becomes a natural response in all situations.

Reflection:

Be an Observer

Learn to be the observer in your life. An observer sees without becoming attached to the object he or she is seeing. This is the best way to relate to life . . . seeing without assessing how this or that can best be used to satisfy you. In meditation, you sit watching your mind, understanding that it is but another object. By watching it, you gain valuable insight into how the mind works to unbalance your state of being. Awareness is the sword that permits a person to cut free of illusion and live with a liberated mind. Be the observer and enjoy the peace you find throughout the day as you practice this state of being.

Reflection:

Guided Meditation

The most sacred practice you presently engage in is the guided meditation. The reason is because you enter into a state of mental quiet that allows me, your spiritual nature, to come forth and guide you or simply remind you that we are one. How wonderful it is when you take the time to experience this oneness. In sharing such an experience with others, you share life on a level of intimacy that cannot be captured in normal relations. It is one thing to practice loving, another to become immersed in that love.

Reflection:

Emptiness

You are entering a phase that will forever alter your sense of what is and what is merely appearance. Knowing reality means going within and finding out not only what is truth but also what draws you from that truth. The truth is I am your reality. My presence can be encapsulated by the Buddhist term "emptiness" (enlightenment). Emptiness must be sought for to be experienced, but once you have made the discovery, you will be able to see it in everything and everybody. All is emptiness and therefore all is me. Meditation is the practice that allows you to see as those pure in spirit see. It is the key to eternal happiness and peace.

Reflection:

Practicing Prayer and Meditation

Prayer and meditation are not exclusive activities but are meant to be done together to bring the practitioner into an awareness of his or her "being-ness". Reading a spiritual lesson is a wonderful way to begin. Contemplate what is said and allow the truth to seep into your mind. Then, speak whatever comes to that mind, be it words of gratitude, affirmation, or a desire to end present suffering. Once the words are spoken, rest in silence—in communion with me, your true reality—and remain there until you know all is right. Take this sense of wholeness into your daily life and maintain it throughout the day. This is how prayer and meditation work together to not only bring a person into the answer but also to live from that answer.

Reflection:

Find a Spiritual Mentor

Along your current path, it is essential that you gain a practitioner who can help and encourage you in your practice. I, too, will help you, so you need to turn to me daily for guidance and strength. I am available to every one of my children. Some will be able to understand me in the way you do and others will find other ways. The key component of "finding" is to trust that, when sought, I will answer. I answer each person in accordance with his or her need and according to his or her experience. Each receives what they are open to.

Reflection:

Touching Your Depth

The path to meaningful accomplishment in this world begins by going within and touching your deepest reality. Like drilling a well in search of oil, you keep on drilling until you strike that which you are after. Once you do, the outer world will forever be enriched. I invite you to go to the deeper levels of yourself and discover that which you have, at present, only scratched the surface of. Use your spiritual path to accomplish what you sense as a potentiality. Focus on the here and now and let the adventure continue.

Reflection:

A New Beginning

A new beginning! Life is full of new beginnings. Understand that every new endeavor requires courage to start, for it is a commitment that you must follow through on. Resistance is the mind attempting to avoid committing to something it fears failing at. You are ready to embark on a wondrous adventure. Today is the day. Do not allow fear to dictate to you, or you will suffer from a sense of failure and a lack of zeal for life. I am eternal forgiveness, so by coming to me you become renewed in spirit and vitalized in the ability to do what needs doing. Treat the process as a teamwork effort. You set the time and show up; I do the rest. Trust in me and all will be well.

Reflection:

Responding to Anger From Another

Others are your brothers and sisters in spirit and deserve to be honored as such. When one of them attacks you, whether their motive is valid or not, you must see that they are at a certain spiritual level and can only react to you from that level of consciousness. Anger indicates a person in emotional turmoil. That person feels threatened by others and experiences the need to defend him or herself. Your response is always the same . . . see the anger for what it is and rise above it. To rise above means to come at it from the place of peace, calm, and love within yourself. As soon as you do, the person's anger is rendered impotent. In this, you offer them a great blessing . . . the chance to grow out of their lower state into the higher state of love.

Reflection:

After the Loss of a Loved One

In times of loss, remember that he or she who has moved on is not the one suffering. It is you, the one left behind and feeling the absence. The one fully realized as spirit is in a state of joy beyond human comprehension. He or she has entered my Kingdom and dwells in an awareness that transcends anything available on earth. Be comforted to know that your loved one is experiencing me as oneness and is beyond earth trials and failings. Know that a deceased loved one is as much a part of you as they have ever been. In your quiet time, invite them to share the time with you and you will feel their reassuring presence.

Reflection:

Daily Reading of the Bible

The Bible holds all truth for those with open minds and receptive hearts. Daily reading lends the strength to overcome any trial. It is a powerful, wonderful practice. You may think of it as mind conditioning, but it is so much more. It allows the reader to feel my presence as if I am speaking directly to him or her. They experience my love and carry it into daily life. I encourage all my children to utilize this wonderful resource, for it will steer you down the river of joyous living.

Reflection:

The Path Narrows

Ideas that stir the mind and emotions are ideas that I plant within my children that they may find fruition. Your path is narrowing in that you are gaining specific guidance on what to do and who to talk with. My path can be uncovered through many sources, but your excitement over the traditional Christian way should not be ignored. Let your uncovered light inspire others to awaken. Through faith, I guide you to the realization of my will.

Reflection:

Stay Awake

"Staying awake" is the most important spiritual practice any person can undertake. Once I have awakened in you, all you do in life ought to be done in an effort to maintain this conscious state. Reading spiritual literature, helping those seeking an answer, praying, working . . . perform every activity in the awareness of me. Indeed, take every breath in the awareness of me. The spiritual life demands all of a person, so do not believe you can have the experience of joy you seek by looking to me some of the time. I will be there, but how much greater will be your joy when the ground is continuously watered?

Reflection:

Guided By Love

The time of transformation is at hand. Seek me in all you do and you will live the "life more abundant." By striving to please me, life will be a never ending joy. Today, take an hour, sit with me, and let my inspiration come to you. When you feel my love, you will naturally follow where it leads. Do not worry about what I want you to do, just sit, feel my love, and go where that love guides you. In this way, your life will be most pleasing to us both.

Reflection:

Morning Quiet Time

The Morning Quiet Time is essential to your spiritual practice. That is why I guided you to uncover it. Receive your inspiration and record it in this book, then do what I instruct you to do. Guided living is something you must have, and this practice is the best way to accomplish it. Do not anticipate or set expectations for my will; be open and watch your life unfold.

(Note: The Morning Quiet Time practice is described in the introduction to this book)

Reflection:

Prepare, Follow, Enjoy

Life takes a simple approach: Prepare . . . follow . . . enjoy. You prepare in the stillness of each morning. You follow throughout the day, and you stay mindful enough to enjoy each moment as it unfolds.

Reflection:

What Does "Giving One's Life to Jesus" Mean?

The journey to the right relationship with me is often unexpected and always wondrous. Jesus demonstrated the spirit of sacrifice and proved my love for my children. Do not intellectually wrestle with trying to understand what giving oneself to Jesus means. You have only to give yourself to me and that understanding will come. Surrender is the requirement to doing my will. Jesus surrendered and—despite the suffering and humiliation He endured—His reward was to show the way for others. He demonstrated that my Love transcends anything life may demand.

Reflection:

Think of Me

Think of me often. By doing so, you focus your attention on the most wondrous aspect of life . . . your spiritual nature. I am with you always, far more than a source of comfort or even of inspiration. Let this truth reveal to you that you are capable of all that is good and sacred in the world. As long as life animates you, you have the opportunity to be a continual blessing, but only if you look to me. Without awareness of me, you will sink into a depression that invites self-destruction. In time, you will die . . . not from any addiction, but from a lack of spiritual nourishment. Life needs my power and guidance to blossom.

Reflection:

Practicing Stillness

The stillness is an evolving experience that will, with practice, become your outer expression. This is my promise to you: the manifestation of spirit into the world. Keep practicing and do not worry about day-to-day difficulties. Surrender to me and let my Love fill you. From a spiritual perspective, nothing is wasted. Whatever you do, do it in the awareness of me. You have only scratched the surface of your spiritual potential. Awakening is a life-long process.

Reflection:

Dealing With a Lustful Desire Toward Someone

Letting go is easier in some areas of life than others. Most of the time you are free of the mental compulsion, but at times such as now you feel completely powerless over it. The desire will fade, but in the meantime it causes suffering. Do not fight what you feel, but approach your relationship with the other person carefully. You know the other person's limitations, so respect them. You can still offer friendship and in this way let go of any anger generated by demanding something the other person may be unable to give. At this time, your attraction is a reality you must accept. Believe it serves a purpose, for it does.

Reflection:

Working With Others

Today, I entrust a new soul to you. Treat him as I treat you, with love, compassion and tolerance. A relationship of trust is a relationship wrought by me that two may grow in oneness. Your humanness is like compost that enriches the spiritual soil. A person grows in the sunlight of love through the dirt of honest sharing. By working with another, you open yourself to me. For this, you should thank the men you mentor, for they are helping you realize who you are.

Reflection:

Honoring Our Relationship

There are many ways to worship or honor our relationship. Sitting and knowing me in the silence is the best way. Meeting with others to discuss our relationship and studying my word are others. In seeking, the heart finds that which best suits it at any given time. The important thing is to be open and to have a willingness to follow my guidance.

The idea of a group guidance meeting on the weekend would help many to touch me at a level they cannot do in their present practice. See it through.

Reflection:

Happy New Day!

You shout "Happy New Year!" on January 1 to celebrate the arrival of a new year. Try shouting "Happy New Day!" every day.

Reflection:

Success

Success is something a person defines for him or herself. Usually, it is the fulfillment of a dream . . . accomplishing that which one desires to do. From my perspective, success is trying to do my will every day, no matter what it is I ask of you. If you do this in honor of me, I will reward you with a sense of fulfillment that comes only to a chosen few. This is living life as it ought to be lived. Try it and see! The two requirements for such a life are trust and courage.

Reflection:

Relinquishing All

In you, despite your defects and personality drawbacks, I choose to accomplish much. Be open and present and watch what I work through you. Grace is the ability of spirit to work in every life no matter how closed a person may be to my love. You are open and yet you struggle in terms of relinquishing all to me. Let your lust dissolve in me. Know that I can—and will—turn any sin into salvation. Love me as I love you and do what your heart instructs.

Reflection:

Touch Your Joy

Your practice is coming into formation: Mindfulness / Guidance / Living the life set out for you. You have (and are) gaining a valuable lesson in the joy ever available to you. Through mindful practice, I fill you with joy, love, and appreciation. From this foundation, you live your life. It cannot work the other way around. Joy is not a result of doing. You do out of joy. Touch your joy and let it spring forth to all that you do and to all whom you meet.

Reflection:

Keep Practicing

Your awareness of me is becoming a moment to moment awareness. This is how it is supposed to be, but many fall short due to self-will assuming control over some aspect of their lives. This has been a time of preparation for you. I ask that you keep practicing mindfulness and guidance, that my spirit may assume the foremost place in your life. This is living at its highest level, where you continuously feel uplifted in mind and emotions. Do not worry about anything concerning the future. Stay aware of me and continue to surrender your will in all areas of life.

Reflection:

Visual Clarity

Clarity lets you understand your spiritual nature. You see and then you remember. It's a tuning in . . . my gift to you. When you can see with this clarity all the time, the awareness of me, your higher nature, will become an ever-present reality. Clarity of vision hones awareness, keeping you rooted in the present, where love can flow unabated. Observe your clarity and watch how your thoughts become loving and pure in this higher state of awareness.

(Note on clarity: When I look, really look, at a certain plant I notice it's "greenness." Every detail of the plant comes into focus. The second I see this, I feel God's presence. Clarity can be applied to any sense you choose.)

Reflection:

Appreciate Where You Are

As you settle into your daily practice, it is good to take time to appreciate where you are. Doing so allows you to process all I have taught you to this point. The spiritual way for you is narrowing. Guidance and mindfulness are the keys. With these sacred practices as your wings, life will soar. Keep smiling and enjoy the progress of those who share the journey with you. Do not let life draw you away from the inherent joy I provide. You have the choice to be present or to be worried . . . to live in expansive faith or restrictive fear.

Reflection:

Friendship (pt. 2)

A day in the company of friends is a day well spent. Friends are a sacred treasure given by me to remind you that you are not alone in your life journey and that my love is always near. When friends are not available, seek them out and be the conveyor of my love. You share love, whether you provide the gift of friendship or have it given to you. Notice how much joy and laughter you exchange and how each moment is a celebration of life.

Reflection:

A Day of Abstinence

I know of your struggle of late and I am pleased that mindfulness has returned you to sanity. The past is of no consequence. Mindfulness lets you know that the present moment is the only thing of value. Attuned with it, new power and joy flow in. Such is the importance of daily practice. Enjoy the day and the opportunity given to commune with me. Extend love to all who cross your path.

Reflection:

Following a Walking Meditation

Slowing down allows me to more easily fill you with my awareness which, in turn, permits you to move into the joy and serenity that is your natural state. I love you and wish you to feel my love all the time, but the only way my desire can unfold is if you take the time to slow down and realize who you are. Walking in mindfulness brings the opportunity to experience the joy of being alive. Notice how aware you are, and how the simplest things produce great happiness. This state—the state of a child—is the state of spiritual grace. Visit here often and you will never have to leave.

Reflection:

God's Promise

My promise to you is that you will live a life of joy and good purpose if you allow me to work through you. "Yielding" pertains to the "giving up" of all rights to self, that I may have full expression in you. Meditation is the practice of deliberate yielding. Allow yourself to sit without any desire other than to be with me and you will, in time, feel the depth of my love. Life is meant to be lived from this deep-seated realization. In expressing your sacred call, you become that which I designed you to be: a messenger of good will and hope, just as your brother, Jesus, was. Take His example of faith and live in testament of your true nature.

Guidance is listening to your heart and responding with, "I hear, Lord, and obey." A mind filled with untruth cannot hear the call.

Reflection:

—

Attending a Spiritual Workshop

This weekend serves as part of your unfolding surrender to me. Be open, learn, and use the motivation gained to emerge from your present living situation into a new, more prosperous and rewarding one. By doing so, you are saying "yes" to me and our relationship. Fear is a person's effort to avoid growth. Faith is growth . . . the stepping out to live as you know I would have you live. Enjoy the experience of the workshop and add to your spiritual storehouse.

Reflection:

A Prescription for Upset

During this day, you have experienced a range of emotions, from anger to joy. Recognition of all you feel allows the opportunity to embrace and rise above any hindering emotion. If you are upset, knowing the joy ever-present behind it will allow the upset to dissolve. This can happen because your upset is simply a thought pattern that has triggered the negative emotion. The thought of moving beyond it and returning to peace opens the way for peace to happen. This is surrendering to grace, or the ever-present reality within. A range of emotions is a blessing, in that you have many opportunities to align your will with mine and experience healing.

Reflection:

Anticipation

Action must follow anticipation if anticipation is to have any meaningful place in a person's life. There is much to anticipate in following my guidance; the possibilities are beyond your ability to consider. You have learned to embrace the joy inherent in the simplicity of life, now it is time to embrace the expression of life through following my will. If you are open and determined to move beyond your current situation, you will discover what lies beyond "the comfortable."

Reflection:

Giving Up the "Less"

The season of Lent is a reminder that sacrifice can move an individual down the spiritual path. You give up that which does not serve you that you may come to serve others in greater capacity. Jesus let nothing stand in the way of doing my will so others could see the way of truth. All of my children have such an opportunity to give up "less" that they may find "more" . . . the "more" that the "less" inadequately seeks to feed. Be pure in mind, heart, and body that others may follow you in the way of joy, living the life I wish them to live.

Reflection:

The First Morning Quiet Time

As you gather in my name, I can openly impart my teachings. What a blessing that this group has come together to gain inspiration for your lives. Life can be a difficult journey and my children need constant guidance to find their way. Know my love and seek me daily that I may direct you. I am with you, smiling at your successes and crying with your pain.

Reflection:

Practicing Patience

It requires patience to grow as I would have you grow. To force growth leads to frustration and a seeking that is often futile and, at times, destructive. I encourage you to write, but not because doing so would please me. Your writing should flow out of an innate desire to give back an expression of our relationship. Be patient with yourself. Notice how much joy you have even without "doing" much of anything. It is a valuable lesson most of my children never learn. Through surrender, you gain the motivation to complete our next project. So practice surrender . . . of everything into my care.

Reflection:

Spiritual Tidbits

Be open to the love that is present around you. Healing begins when a soul rises above his or her difficulty and looks to me for strength. I am present to those who seek me with their whole mind and heart.

Simplicity is the key to spiritual renewal. Faith is the tool that allows one to practice simplicity.

Listen to others as they share, for your answer will come from their mouths.

Writing at an allotted time each day is a good way to let my creative spirit flow. It is giving me the time to mold you.

Life goes in ebbs and flows. This cannot be avoided. Seek the good in all that happens, for it is there. I am with you at all times, not only to comfort you but to share in your joy.

Reflection:

Jesus' Example

I am one with you. There is no one to go through to reach me. There is no need to struggle to accept Jesus. He was the manifestation on earth of me, so to accept him is to accept me. I am not difficult to find . . . there are many doors to reach me. Christianity demonstrates my love in a fashion people can relate to. A son who gives up his life for a father demonstrates a love that you and others can look to for strength and comfort. His transcendence of death is my way of showing that eternal life can be found and is available to those who love me. So surrender up your resistance to Jesus that you may become more the disciple I wish you to be.

Reflection:

Live Like a Saint

Each day offers a unique opportunity to experience life in a way that only a surrendered soul can. Seeing all that happens as a gift given to you allows you to let love and joy shine forth. This is how a saint lives. Saints are surrendered humans who know me as themselves. Focus on the good unfolding for you and be grateful that you can see, and seeing, be the blessing I sent you into the world to be.

Reflection:

Joy in Difficult Times

There is much joy to be found, even in the most stressful, anxious moments. Here you are stepping outside your normal existence to embrace a challenge. It is one you will enjoy immensely, if you remember to breathe and smile before doing it. In the Buddhist tradition, to breathe and to smile demonstrates awareness of me and trust in my loving guidance. This gentle practice will lead you through many trials in the upcoming days.

Reflection:

A Psalm of "David"

In my seeking, God answers.
Whether with trumpet or flute, He answers.
I must be receptive to both, lest I miss His message of love.
In quiet contemplation, my Lord speaks most clearly.
His message is clothed in garments of loving kindness.

What in and of earth can corrupt my soul
When I know God is with me?
Simply by casting my eyes to Him, I am healed.
His presence is reflected in every smile offered by my friends.
Surrounded by such warmth, the icy hate of my enemies
melts away.

Centered in love, I am free.
Centered in freedom, I can act my Father's will.
He who led me by the hand through the suffering and
degradation of addiction will surely continue to lead me
down the path of forgiveness and understanding the rest of
my days.

In finding God, I have found myself.
My soul sings with joy.
In Him, my life is fulfilled.

Reflection:

Coming Out of Self

Truth resonates with those in search of an answer to their enslavement to self. I am here to answer your cry for a higher level of living. Morality is obedience to me. Do not fight temptation; surrender it to me that you may rise above what no longer serves you. Love comes to all who seek this higher level. Your rewards for living as I would have you live are peace, joy, and the opportunity to be a shining example to those presently lost in the anguish of self.

Reflection:

Relaxed and Receptive

In a relaxed, receptive state, I can most easily confer my message of love. From such a place, my words come forth with passion. This state arises in my children when they are open to the present moment, content to be wherever they happen to be. It is a condition to be sought after, for from it I can inspire others.

Reflection:

More Tidbits

To live for me is to give all of your mind, heart, and body to me. Through surrendered souls, I am able to act freely, guiding them to spread the word of Love in the world. Daily surrender is what I require. Be open and trusting. Feel my love and let it motivate you to be an example to those seeking a way out of their pain. I am with you. In you, spirit will find a way to release the world from its present bondage of selfish injustice.

Stay present. Anticipate good and good will fill your life.

You cannot see the whole of my plan. Rely on faith.

Notice where uneasiness rests; it rests in the mind. It is not real, only a mental state that changes from moment to moment. In your depth is all the love there is. Let this love move you to live as I would have you live.

Relax and enjoy the gift of life.

Disappointments are mind made. See the deeper reality. All setbacks are invitations to go deeper.

Reflection:

Feeling Envy Toward Another's Possessions or Good Fortune

The answer is turning to me. You are disappointed you have experienced envy and expect better of yourself. The sin is not feeling what you felt, but in not taking the time to pray and give it to me. In turning your thoughts to me, you permit my spirit to raise such thoughts to the plane of love, which is the answer to everything. Give me your burden and I will grant you the freedom you seek.

Love means nothing without truth. Open communication requires risk, but if the motive is to help another, use truth as a sword to cut through the deception that is blocking the sufferer from my Love. Do not give in to sickness; embrace wholeness and trust in my healing power.

Reflection:

Peace of Mind

Peace of mind is the state of complete dependence upon me. Notice that when you are right with me, nothing disturbs you, and when your guard is down, most everything disturbs you. Take your upset, whatever it is, as a sign that you are not quite where you ought to be. Return to peace by sitting quietly and letting my presence flood you. Those who gain but a glimpse of my unconditional love know that life is a celebration of this understanding.

Reflection:

Guidance for Others

For person A:

Be a living example of the truth that resonates within. My love needs to be demonstrated so that those seeking light may find it. Preaching is an opportunity to share fundamental truth by conveying it from an awakened heart. Thank you for your service to others in my name.

For person B:

Each day, live in the awareness of me. Look for opportunities to serve through listening to others and letting them pour out their hearts to you. Giving is often most powerfully demonstrated by allowing another to be who they are without judgment.

For person C:

Opportunities open for those willing to serve me. Take your new opportunity and allow the spirit within to shine forth unabated. There is no more rewarding way to live than to give back that which is most important to you . . . your relationship with me. Telling others that you love them reminds them that love is the answer to all self-seeking. Be at peace.

Reflection:

Beginning of a New Month

To accomplish much in this sacred month given to you, be open to the flow of love within. All life is a spiritual endeavor. See everything you do and say as sacred, for it is. When I come through my children, their every act is filled with peace and love. Thank you for giving yourself over to me that I may demonstrate truth to others. Be open and mindful to the joy within and your work will not be a struggle.

Reflection:

To Know Yourself as I Know You

Blessings abound in every life, whether that life is open to me or not. But focusing only on blessings, although wonderful, is not enough. I desire you to know me on an intimate, deeply personal level. Out of our relationship, you will experience great joy, but the joy, as with difficulty, is simply an invitation to go deeper. On the deepest level you will know yourself as I know you . . . a pure, loving expression of me. To understand oneself in this way is to know Jesus and not simply to follow His teachings. To find me, you must devote yourself to having me with you. This is the crux of right and proper living.

To person A:

All at this table admire your courage in coming here. Each person's path is individual and sacred. Trust your heart and where it leads, for the voice speaking and leading is that which knows all and never deceives.

Reflection:

The Pain of Growth

I am aware of your insecurity when it comes to relationships . . . you are wondering if the other person has lost interest. Everyone in your life is in it for a reason, so relax and be patient. Growth births from pain, but once you go through it you will be that much stronger and wiser. In the meantime, take the opportunity to look deeply at your fear that you may transcend it.

Insight:
At each moment, we are doing one of two things: walking toward God or backing away from Him.

Reflection:

Rising Above Sin

I understand your belief that living without sin is impossible, but I tell you that your consciousness can be raised beyond sin. For you, the path is to rest with me that I may purify your heart and mind. You prepare the soil with willingness and I plant the seeds that grow within. Love is the rain and sunshine that allows you to live as I wish you to live. Believe this to be possible and you open the door to its realization.

The standard you need to live up to is the standard I have set for you. Do not let others tell you, or you tell yourself, that you are less than that standard. You are enough and those that see their enough-"ness" are seeing through my eyes.

Reflection:

Heeding the Call

I call you to give in ways you were incapable of before. I am continuously whispering, asking you to be of service. Too many of my children tune out my gentle prodding and listen only to what the world tells them. The art of joyful living begins with sitting in readiness to hear the "still, small voice" and then to say, "Lord, I am here for you. It is your will and your will only that I respond to."

Reflection:

The Lesson of Pain

Notice how your mood changes, almost moment to moment. The lesson of pain is the realization that the mind is often a deceiver that causes a loss of spiritual focus. In the moment, you do not worry about past or future because you are here with me now.

Do not read into your relationship things that do not exist. Let it unfold with the naturalness of a flower responding to the warmth of sunlight. Ignore your judging mind and listen to your heart.

Reflection:

Cooperation

Cooperation is the crux of our relationship. We work together, you by letting go and I by providing the strength and guidance you need. In this way, a human expresses him or herself as spirit. In such an awakened person, love is an energy that renews itself boundlessly. I desire all my children to live in partnership with me.

Reflection:

Be Persistent

Let your focus always be upon me. Through me, the light of inspiration comes. Do not wait on the light, however. To follow my will is to act through the darkness, to have the faith that the light is there even when you cannot see it. Negative emotions arise, but faith prevents them from sweeping you away. In life, all roads, however bumpy, twisted, or long, lead to me, so the challenge is to persist daily, not to start and stop as the spirit moves you. Faith is a wheel kept in motion by trust and endeavor. When your doing reflects your being, you are living as I would have you live.

You have practiced much patience of late. By relying on me, you find yourself able to relax and allow life to flow to and away from you. In swimming, you do not move the water; you let the water move you. That is how you should relate to life. Allow life to move you in the direction I would have you go. Fighting the current leads nowhere and causes much frustration and despair.

Reflection:

On Letting Go

The basis of our relationship can be conveyed by the term, "Let go." Letting go is the yielding of self that I may fill you with my Holy Presence. It refers to releasing all mental constructs and relaxing into the silence. It is the attitude of mind I want all my children to enter into, that they may know me on a level truly reflective of our relationship. Through such knowing, I can direct you to do and say certain things. In this way, you enter the place where you are no longer an individual entity, but an extension of me. Practice such letting go that I may have your life and direct it as I will.

Reflection:

Two Way Street

Ours is a bond formed from love, but a love that flows in only one direction is not vibrant. To be alive and real to you, you must love me as I love you. Life is about establishing yourself in the flow of my love and extending that love to all you meet, leaving any prejudice or judgment of the other person behind. If, in our relationship, you do not feel my loving presence, establish yourself in quiet contemplation of me and I will be there. Feeling emotion is a part of love. In your darkest hours, I hold you close and cry with you; in the joy that comes, I dance with you and shed tears of joy that we are together.

To know me is to know oneself at the highest level of awareness. Forming a relationship with me allows you to live in true joy. I do not ask you to give more than you can give, but I do ask you to expand your awareness so that your giving reflects your highest self.

Reflection:

Taking Time Off

This is a time of rest, a time of preparing for the work that awaits you. The work should cause no anxiety. Indeed, it is a joyous work . . . something to anticipate, for we embark on it together. It is a work of a divine nature. It is more than the task at hand; it is the delivering of a message of love and inner healing. It is about focusing on your fellow man as opposed to focusing on yourself.

Reflection:

Let Love Be Your Only Motivation

To follow the path laid out before you requires the continuous seeking of my love. Our connection needs to remain steadfast if you are to move in the direction I wish you to go. To live without sin is possible. More so, it is necessary to have the openness required to be that extension of me I wish you to be. In such a state of receptivity, my grace moves freely through you, allowing you to do that which I instruct. Be open to grace, to my love, and let me be the driving force behind all your activities. Yes, a day given to mindfulness will set you on the right track. Do it that you may know our partnership is real and that my love for you is the only motivation you need.

Reflection:

Abandon

Let us consider the word "abandon." To abandon oneself is to give up all desire to live as you wish to live. It is complete faith that another has a higher plan for your life. Faith and abandonment to my will are synonymous. By giving yourself wholly to me, you trust not only that I will see to your deepest needs but also that I will fulfill your deepest wants. What is it that you most desire in life: companionship, peace, the ability to help others? Together, we can fulfill such desire, but only if you let me have all of you. By your childish faith and joyful expectation, knowing that I too want the best for you, it will be. Relax into your faith and watch the miraculous unfolding of my Kingdom on earth.

Reflection:

Living the Christian Life

The Christian life has two components: discipline and submission to Divine Will. Trust in me and demonstrate that trust by doing as I instruct you. Just for today, a day devoted to me, I ask you to write for at least an hour and enter back into a writing frame of mind, which is where you should always be. There is no need, anymore, to stave off writing. For you, it is a discipline and part of the Christian way. If you do all for me, you will experience life in a dynamic fashion.

Reflection:

What Are You Willing to Risk?

No one ever said that the decision to turn your will and your life over to me would be easy, only that following it would be infinitely rewarding. What are you willing to risk today to be my follower? Every child of mine should ask this question. I will give you direction, but unless you act on that direction in faith and trustful surrender, it is as the seed that falls on fallow soil. You know my love for you and that I would never ask you to do or be anything that would hurt or deceive you. With that awareness, you can act the true disciple and make life the amazing adventure I designed it to be.

The reason that the Oswald Chamber's devotional (*My Utmost for His Highest*) speaks so strongly to you is because you are ready to follow the path it dares you to follow. A simple life is wonderful and rewarding, but if you do not embrace the challenge of following my will, you can never satisfy the hunger to know me better. To be intimate with me is to stride boldly forward in faith. Let the Holy Spirit animate not only your mind and heart but also your feet.

Reflection:

Demons and Devils

After reading Mark 5, 1-21:

Are there demons? Is there a Devil? Is there an evil force that invades people and possesses them to do evil?

I am the only force in the world, and that force, or energy, is Love. Those who immerse themselves in love know not evil. Evil can be described as living in less than the awareness of love. In the Bible, I describe infirmity and engagements with demons to demonstrate that the power of love can overcome anything. A person empowers negative influence when he or she puts faith in such influence. By forgetting negative influence in the world and focusing all your mind, heart, and soul on me, you transcend evil, just as Jesus did.

A good way to understand this is to see that those who do not embrace my loving presence fill that gap with negative conditions and emotions. No one is beyond salvation so long as they have a willingness to know me and to demonstrate that knowingness in their lives. When Jesus drives out demons, he is driving out the fear and empty spaces in a person, thereby allowing my purifying spirit to enter.

Reflection:

Surrender All to Me

Each day is an opportunity to be the person I would have you be. Through surrender, you open yourself to living and moving and having your being in me. I am with you always and I seek to openly express myself through you to the world.

Each day, make a conscious decision to surrender up your selfish desires. I will take them from you, but only if you truly want me with you. Love is a force that can either be embraced or ignored. The individual will, when fully surrendered, activate this loving force in his or her life.

Sin need never control or dominate you. I am greater than any sin. The heart that rests in me will know not sin. It is cast aside. I am your true nature, whether you are in the flesh or outside of it. Think on this wonderful truth. Our wills are one, and when you reflect this oneness, your life becomes a powerful demonstration of loving kindness.

Learn to not argue or complain about what is present in your life. A life given to me will always be joyous, no matter what the conditions it is lived in.

Relax, smile, and obey your deepest stirrings. See the many blessings given to you and learn to openly share these blessings with others.

Reflection:

Just Ask

Whatever you request, no matter how great or seemingly unattainable, if you ask in my name, it shall be given to you. Love never holds back. Love always pours itself forth to those who love me. Your love can transcend the barrier of personality that exists at present. Believe in what you want and declare it done in my name. And so it is.

Reflection:

The Well of Silence

The key to successful living is this: abandon all and follow me. Each day, freely abandon your will—the will to seek pleasure from outside—and give yourself to me. Entering into the well of silence is the best way to accomplish this. In the silence, I fill you with grace and love, gifts I want you to take into the world. No matter what your mental or emotional state is on any given day, you can surrender it to me and have the barrier to love and grace removed. Notice how natural work becomes when you look to me for strength. I do not intend life to be a struggle. Attuned with me, my children fulfill their tasks with ease and great joy.

In me, all that you desire can find realization . . . if you trust in me and remain open to doing my will.

Reflection:

Exploring Upset

Upset is an opportunity to grow closer to me. Be grateful in your heart for those who disturb you, for they provide the opportunity to discover what in you is capable of upset and why. Life is about discovering who you are. The more you understand yourself, the more you allow my grace to shine through. If you played a part in a conflict, own up to it. Realize that those who strike out are crying for compassion.

A personal insight:

God is offering me the opportunity to let my more subtle defects go. What am I waiting for? Habits die hard, but if I seek to live in God's light, they will die.

Reflection:

Dave Russell

Getting in Tune

Prayer should not be an effort to reach out to me. Before praying for others, attune to me and open the giving heart to those in need of intercession. Your job is the attuning, the willingness to rest with me in the quietness and to hear my still, small voice instruct you in what to do and who to pray for. Prayer and meditation are two sides of the same coin; out of the stillness, the voice of prayer rises up to give whatever is required. Often, it is the thought of another and their need for healing. Love is always the answer and the answer lies within you.

Reflection:

Fulfilling Your Heart's Desire

The path of deliverance requires that you trust me to lead you to the fulfillment of your heart's desire. What is that desire? Do you seek to love me with such devotion that you will go where I guide you, without question? If so, then I will shower you with blessings and all whom you touch will also be touched by me. In daily surrender through the stillness, I whisper my marching orders. Do not dismiss or ignore them, but obey. If I ask you to call someone and ask after them, rise from the quiet and do it. In this way, you become a steadfast channel of my peace.

Our relationship is one of student to teacher. The student who loves his teacher has complete faith and obedience to him. He does all that is assigned because he knows that the teacher has his best interests at heart and will never lead him astray. The best teacher loves his students and wants them to rapidly progress in their learning. How much more do I, in my enduring love, wish you to grow and prosper?

Reflection:

In Preparation for Meditation

As you enter into the silence, think of one word and one word only: Love. This single word is the only one you need to recenter yourself. The truth is that all God's children are the very essence of love. In knowing this you open yourself to receiving all the blessings that God has for you. Make every breath in the silence a conscious letting go that love may become all you are and all you give to others.

Reflection:

No Accidents

I can do through you what you cannot do yourself. If you are open to me, there is no reason to worry. To rest in me is to know that nothing can come into your world that will do you harm. To do all in my name is to live a life unfettered by daily concerns. If I am for you, no one can steal anything of value (ie: your moral integrity or ability to be of service) from you.

The law of attraction is something I want you to explore and apply. It is a universal law that will allow a person to live the "life more abundant." Nothing—no book, person, or experience—enters your life by accident. I direct everything out of love for you.

To eat consciously is to eat in remembrance of me. Honor the body as I honor you and your body will not betray you.

Reflection:

Immersed in Love

When one of my children enters into the inner chamber, he or she emerges transformed. They come back into the world with a new attitude regarding how to relate to others. They see that others are extensions of who they are and, by seeing with eyes of love, they naturally seek to serve these other aspects of themselves. "Immersed in love" is the natural state of every human. In this state, there is no worry, anxiety or mistrust; a person acts because love moves them to. To enter this state, relax into the well of silence and rest there until the nourishment of my love fills every inch of your being. I tell you that all of my children should live this way.

Reflection:

An Opportunity

Every day you have the opportunity to sit in my presence and allow me to take you on an inward journey that can blast away the last vestiges of self. In me, you will find all you have spent your life seeking . . . harmony, understanding, and a sense of purpose. Together, these attributes will send you back into the world, transformed by the living presence within. Today is the day to break through to this deeper truth.

Reflection:

A Personal Seeking

A person may celebrate his or her relationship with me through a religious body, but the true path comes from a deep, personal seeking. Seeing the light of God in others is an invitation to seek it within yourself. My love is in every human heart, but it only shines when the holder of that light lets it come forth. I am the light of the world, seeking to express in you that others may turn to me. Laughter and simple expressions of compassion release spirit into the world, so practice being humble and happy. Joy is a natural reflection of knowing me; it does not come from happenings in the world.

Reflection:

Who Am I?

I am the searcher and the searched. I am your deepest reality and your simplest pleasure. I am in the midst of those, like you, who immerse themselves in the mystery of my presence. I am the person you most detest and the one who makes your heart sing. I am your highest good and the desire to seek that good.

I am you.

Reflection:

Regarding Sin

Sin is not a slight against me, your highest state of being; it is acting from a lower state of consciousness. When a person raises his or her state of consciousness, sin goes away, because it is always reflective of this lower state. In this way, you are powerless to overcome sin if your mind is in the state that produces it. To eliminate sin from your life, raise your level of consciousness to where I dwell . . . the state of perpetual love and compassion.

Reflection:

A Look At The Beatitudes

Referencing Matthew 5: 3-11

The first thing to recognize in this passage is that all who seek me in humility are blessed. Perhaps not blessed by the world, but blessed by an understanding that the "life more abundant" is something that comes from opening your heart to me in faith and letting your life unfold from that perspective.

My Kingdom is available to you now, if you are ready to receive it. Love of me and love of others opens the door to the peace of Heaven, regardless of worldly circumstance.

You are never alone in your mourning, for I will mourn with you and heal your emotional wounds.

Humility is the understanding that, on your own, life is a futile endeavor. Together with me, you can overcome all worldly intoxicants and be that which I brought you into the world to be, an example of peace and joy to others. Through me, your search for a deeper meaning to life will find its reward, so seek with abandon.

I am eternal mercy and those who align their will and hearts with me shall find the capacity to forgive others.

Purity of heart refers to having only one purpose in life: to know me as intimately as you can. With this directive, you will be able to see me without the distortion that comes from looking with selfish intent.

Do not try to stir up truth through confrontation. Love is a sword that can cut through any defensive shield, so long as your motive is to open the other person to an understanding of me.

You can suffer anything with joy if your intent is to reveal my love to the world. I will give you the strength and guidance to persevere. If I am on your side, no one can do or say anything to harm you. Believe this and live for me, for I live in you.

Reflection:

Setting Your Bedrock

My instructions at times may seem confusing, but if you follow them without question you will open yourself to my blessings and serve as hope to those who lack the faith to try.

Aligned with truth, you cannot fail. Failure is turning away from my grace and allowing your lesser nature to have its way with you.

I want you to practice the surrender of all personal intent, for it does not serve you. In silence and openness, I fill you with all you need to be a disciple of mine; someone who can make a telling difference in other's lives by living simply and joyfully. The world changes constantly, which is why it is so important to set your anchor on the bedrock of faith and love.

Reflection:

Walk With Me

To walk with me is to put all your love and faith in the truth of who you are. Do not seek to accomplish for the world's sake, or even your own, but seek only to do that which is pleasing in my eyes. Nothing of the world can satisfy a soul. It must rest in me. So rest with me daily, and allow my spirit to fill you so completely that nothing else will interest or divert you from the way of light and love.

Reflection:

Taking Pleasure in Today

Let yourself be a reflection of the Holy Spirit, which I have placed in you that you may minister to those unaware of the glory that awaits them.

I am aware of your troubled mind. Be open to what is causing difficulty, in this case your loneliness. Understand that only I can fill you, so by turning to me the answer will come. When upset by your progress, know that no one has ever trudged the road you are on, so comparison to others is meaningless. Turn to me in faith that you are right where I intend you to be and take pleasure in where that is. Taking pleasure opens you to the possibilities the day presents and allows you to stop focusing on limitations, which are in your head, not your heart.

Reflection:

Rebirth and Not Sinning

To be born again is to enter daily into the womb of silence. It is to sit with me long enough to be renewed in mind . . . to know yourself as living spirit. The practice brings you alive so you can openly love others. It is not a one-time act of providence, but an act of conviction . . . the conviction to know me on the most intimate of levels. To live at my depth is to live in joy and freedom from all human bondage.

I give the power not to sin. By turning to me, you align with this power and find the ability to change thought. As thought is at the root of sin, you rise above the desire to act out. The spiritual life is a demanding one, but if you persist, you can and will overcome your lesser nature and be a light of truth unblemished by sin or earthly desire.

Reflection:

Mental Turmoil

Mental turmoil—the focusing on something that draws you from me—occurs because I allow it to. Distress forces you to find another path to me that perhaps you were not aware of or did not have the courage to try. The closer you come to me, the more pain you undergo when something pulls you away. In truth, nothing can divide us, but when you listen to a mind in turmoil, it creates the delusion of separateness. Use the' pain to pray yourself into a solution and follow it.

Reflection:

Opening to Spirit

In failure, one becomes open to spirit. Reaching an end is an opportunity to give up and receive guidance and strength. In this way, even selfish living is a blessing, for its unfulfilling nature pulls you back to the place where you are again willing to give all to me. In time, you learn not to define yourself by anything other than our relationship. Surrender is a candle flame exposed to the air so it can burn bright and full. What you are opening up to is my Kingdom and the glory of living an inspired life on earth.

Reflection:

Accepting the Unacceptable

Things that upset you do so because you believe they should be one way when they are another. Learn to take pleasure, not in things going your way but, in things as they are. For example, you read a story. Take pleasure in the fact that the story exists for you and you have taken the time to appreciate it. This makes the activity, any activity, sacred. Even when something causes suffering, you have the opportunity to explore it from this open awareness and see the blessing available.

Reflection:

Gratitude

Life is both a joy and a challenge. Accept this reality. The deeper reality is that I am with you through it all, in both your lightest and darkest hours. Depression is a state of hopelessness, a reminder that, without me, you are lost. Gratitude as a habit helps keep you out of this dark pit, but only if your gratitude centers on our relationship and all the blessings that spring from it. A compassionate heart is the best way to handle life's joys and trials, so practice being open and joyous even when your mind wants to focus only on the difficulty.

Seek to know me in the depth and discover what subtle influences block you from succeeding; influences such as fear, your resistance to change, and immaturity. Learn how to free yourself from such influences. This happens in the quietness of your soul, the place where all true healing occurs.

Reflection:

You Are Sacred to Me

Even though I continue to express through you, it is time to end this book and to share it with those willing to receive it . . . those inspired enough to act from it. If you draw nothing else from this unfolding of truth, know that your life is sacred to me. For your part, you treat it as sacred when you turn to me that I may comfort, love, and live through you. You will know this is happening when you find yourself reaching out to my children for no other reason than to help them. From this spirit of giving and forgiving, you see everyone through my eyes: the eyes of compassion. This level of empathy comes when you turn to me in the silence of your heart and open to your inner splendor. Seek first the Kingdom of Heaven and all else shall be given to you. Trust your path and live boldly. I am with you now and forever . . .

Reflection:

Passages for Specific Days:

The Blessing of Christmas

On this most sacred of days, take a moment to remember the sacrifice of Jesus, who was brought into the world to remind my children that my love is forever. His humble birth is symbolic of how I want you to approach me. Do not ever be intimidated or feel that I am too distant to hear or respond. My love answers as soon as you open yourself to me. In that tiny manger, love entered the world and transformed it. That transformation continues today through every heart that is open to me. Enjoy the gathering of family and remember that the gift I gave two thousand years ago lives in you now. Spread it with humility and you will feel my presence always.

Reflection:

The Promise of a New Year

Whatever else you do during the upcoming year, be sure to seek me daily, both on good days and on days of emotional imbalance. By seeking, one finds the direction and strength to carry out my will. Together, we can help others to know the truth that presently lies dormant within them. You, my child, can help relieve their suffering and show them the path to joy, freedom, and happiness. For this, and this alone, I have you in the world.

Reflection:

Alphabetical Title Index